12 MINUTE WORKOUT

By **Pete Muir**

Photography **Tom Miles**
Model **Mark Hughes@WAthletic**
Design **Ian Jackson**
Subeditor **Matthew Hurrell**

Equipment supplied by **www.fitness-superstore.co.uk**

Digital Production Manager **Nicky Baker**
Bookazine Manager **Dharmesh Mistry**
Production Director **Robin Ryan**
Managing Director of Advertising
Julian Lloyd-Evans
Newstrade Director **Martin Belson**
Chief Operating Officer **Brett Reynolds**
Group Finance Director **Ian Leggett**
Chief Executive **James Tye**
Chairman **Felix Dennis**

The 'Magbook' brand is a trademark of Dennis Publishing Ltd,
30 Cle.. in England.
All n..),
a...

To ....
+44 (0) 20 7907 6134 or email ornella_roccoletti@dennis.co.uk

reflex®

INSTANT WHEY DELUXE

A NEW VARIANT OF INSTANT WHEY WITH AN UNBEATEN TASTE

FLAVOUR & PERFORMANCE

Instant Whey Deluxe combines an unbeaten taste with a competitive protein level. By using specially selected protein that is rich in peptides and amino acids which are more readily absorbed in the body compared to bonded proteins, an almost instantaneous hit of muscle building amino acids is provided.

It also contains glutamine which has been studied for its unique contribution to protein synthesis, its ability to help prevent muscle tissue breakdown as well as supporting the immune system and assisting cell hydration and volume.

WITH HEALTH FOCUSED INGREDIENTS

Not only does Instant Whey Deluxe combine an unbeaten taste with a competitive protein level, but it also contains health focused ingredients with the inclusion of Digezyme enzymes and Lactospore probiotics. Digezyme enzymes have been shown to enhance protein digestion, whilst Lactospore probiotics, similar to those found in certain yoghurts, provide for a healthier gut.

Instant Whey Deluxe is naturally rich in cysteine which helps promote the body's natural production of Glutathione which is a master antioxidant.

PERFORMANCE & HEALTH WITHIN

SYNERGY BIO ®

Make it Happen!

REACH YOUR
GOALS
WITH OUR AWARD
WINNING PRODUCTS

Ben Noy

MODEL & BIO-SYNERGY CUSTOMER

Foreword

MINUTE WORKOUT

At *Men's Fitness* magazine we get a lot of letters and emails from readers, and many of them say the same thing: 'I just can't find the time to train properly!'

People are busy. You have to juggle work, home, family and social commitments, and you don't want to have to give any of them up in order to spend an hour in the gym several times a week. But you do want to look good, feel energised and protect your health.

So what can you do?

The answer is not to train harder, but to train smarter. Many men waste hours in the gym simply wandering around, waiting for equipment or training in a way that is ineffective. The truth is you don't need an hour-long workout to get fit and lean. By following routines that maximise your body's response to the training stimuli, you can torch fat, add new muscle and get an effective cardiovascular workout in just 12 minutes.

That doesn't mean these workouts are easy – some of them will test even seasoned athletes – but they are all very efficient and they get results.

Try one today. You may discover that you have more free time than you realised.

Pete Muir, Editorial Director, *Men's Fitness*

CONTENTS

8-13
Tip & Terms

Everything you need to get you started

15-69
The Workouts

27 effective routines – all 12 minutes long

71-127
Form Guides

How to perform each exercise perfectly

HOW TO USE THIS GUIDE

Have you got 12 minutes spare to do a workout?

There are 27 of them for you to choose from in this guide

Here are a few of the things you should consider when selecting which workout to do:

■ **What level of fitness are you at?**

■ **What equipment do you have available?**

■ **What is the main effect you want the workout to have?**

Use the information on the left-hand side of each workout to guide you in making your choice. You don't need to start at Workout 1. You can pick and choose to suit your needs, or even create your own workouts based on the exercises and formats that you learn about in this guide. You can try a different workout each time, or aim to improve your performance in a particular workout.

Whichever workout you go for, be sure to follow the form guides and train within your ability.

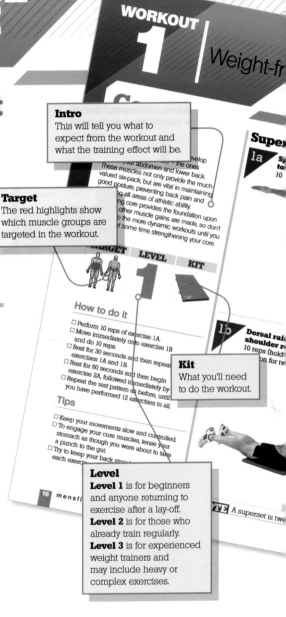

WORKOUT 1 Weight-fr

Intro
This will tell you what to expect from the workout and what the training effect will be.

Super
1a

...velop
...our abdomen and lower back.
These muscles not only provide the much-
valued six-pack, but are vital in maintaining
good posture, preventing back pain and
...g all areas of athletic ability.
...ng core provides the foundation upon
other muscle gains are made, so don't
...o the more dynamic workouts until you
...t some time strengthening your core.

Target
The red highlights show which muscle groups are targeted in the workout.

TARGET   LEVEL   KIT

How to do it
☐ Perform 10 reps of exercise 1A.
☐ Move immediately onto exercise 1B and do 10 reps.
☐ Rest for 30 seconds and then repeat exercises 1A and 1B.
☐ Rest for 60 seconds and then begin exercise 2A, followed immediately by you have performed 12 exercises in all.
☐ Repeat the rest pattern as before, until you have performed 12 exercises in all.

1b **Dorsal rai shoulder r**
10 reps (hold
...n for tw

Kit
What you'll need to do the workout.

Tips
☐ Keep your movements slow and controlled.
☐ To engage your core muscles, tense your stomach as though you were about to take a punch to the gut.
☐ Try to keep your back stra...
each exerc...

Level
Level 1 is for beginners and anyone returning to exercise after a lay-off.
Level 2 is for those who already train regularly.
Level 3 is for experienced weight trainers and may include heavy or complex exercises.

YTE A superset is twe

16 mensfi

12 MINUTE WORKOUT

Do this

This is an abbreviated description of how to perform the workout. A longer description is in the left-hand panel, marked 'How to do it'.

DO THIS

- 2 supersets for each group
- Rest 30 secs between supersets
- Rest 60 secs between groups

12 MINUTE WORKOUT

...ing feet with each rep)

...rm guide: p88

Superset 2

2a

Side lunge woodchop
10 reps (5 reps each side)

Superset 3

3a

Lunge with rotation
10 reps (alternate sides with each rep)

Exercises

Each image shows one part of the exercise. If you need a fuller explanation of how to perform it, find it in the Form Guides section.

...ge
...ps each sid

Form guide: p8...

Form Guides

The page number of the form guide for each exercise is located at the bottom of the exercise. The form guides give detailed explanations on how to perform each exercise correctly and safely.

...idge

Form guide: p81

: p92

...one back

-to-back with no rest f...

FORM GUIDES

12 MINUTE WORKOUT

BARBELL LUNGE

LUNGE WITH ROTATION

LUNGE TO CURL

DUMB-BELL LUNGE WITH ROTATION

mensfitness.co.uk

GLOSSARY

Some terms you'll find throughout this book

Workout
A series of exercises performed with a specific goal.

Circuit
A type of workout where exercises are performed back-to-back with no rest in between.

Rep
Short for repetition, a single execution of a particular exercise.

Set
A specific number of reps.

Superset
Two sets of different exercises performed back-to-back with no rest in between.

Rest
The time taken between sets to recover before beginning again.

Core
The muscles of your midsection, including abdominals and lower back.

Failure
The point at which you can't complete another rep without compromising good form.

Tempo
The speed of movement of an exercise. A change in tempo will alter the effect of an exercise.

Compound
An exercise that uses multiple joint movements and muscles groups at the same time.

Isolation
An exercise that uses single joint movements and targets a specific muscle group.

Plyometric
An exercise that uses dynamic, explosive movements such as jumps or fast lifts.

Eccentric
The portion of a lift where the muscle lengthens under resistance (the lowering portion).

Concentric
The portion of a lift where the muscle shortens under resistance (the lifting portion).

Resistance
The force that works against a muscle during exercise.

Stability
An exercise that requires your muscles to hold your body in a stable, balanced position.

Free weights
Weights, such as dumb-bells and barbells, that are not restricted in their usage or path of motion (as opposed to exercise machines that only allow the user to exercise in a particular manner).

Splits
The way a workout routine is divided, usually by different body parts or movement patterns.

Spotter
Somebody who assists you during heavy lifts by taking control of the weight when you hit failure.

Cardio
Short for 'cardiovascular', it refers to exercise that is designed to strengthen the heart and improve general fitness.

KIT ROUNDUP

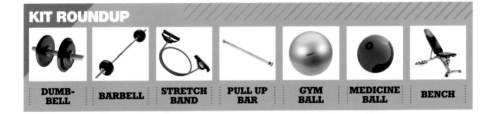

| DUMB-BELL | BARBELL | STRETCH BAND | PULL UP BAR | GYM BALL | MEDICINE BALL | BENCH |

12 MINUTE WORKOUT

MAIN MUSCLE GROUPS

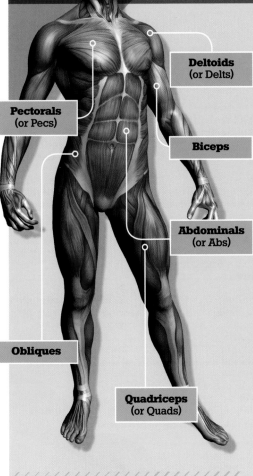

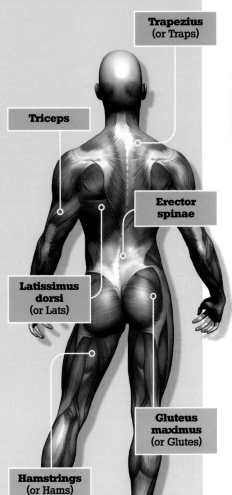

Trapezius (or Traps)

Deltoids (or Delts)

Pectorals (or Pecs)

Triceps

Biceps

Erector spinae

Abdominals (or Abs)

Latissimus dorsi (or Lats)

Obliques

Gluteus maximus (or Glutes)

Quadriceps (or Quads)

Hamstrings (or Hams)

TRAINING TIPS

Get the most from your workouts
A few things to keep in mind before you begin

Get checked out
If you have any worries at all about your readiness, get yourself checked by a GP, especially if you have a history of heart trouble.

Warm-up properly
Before doing any of the workouts, raise your body temperature by doing gentle cardio work, such as running or cycling, and prepare your muscles by doing squats, bends and presses. It will help to prevent strains or muscle tears.

Stretch afterwards
Stretching helps flush lactic acid out of your muscles, which can prevent some muscle soreness. Good flexibility also allows you to work your muscles through a bigger range of motion, which will help you to get fitter and stronger faster.

Listen to your body
If you feel pain at any time during your workout, stop immediately. Don't work through it – you could do serious damage to muscles, joints or tendons.

Watch your form
Check the form guides for each exercise and follow them to the letter. Good form will not only help you to avoid injury, but will ensure the best results in terms of your fitness gains.

Choose the right weight
Pick a weight you can manage easily the first time you perform any lifting exercise. This way you can focus on performing the exercise perfectly, then build up the weight once you've mastered the move. The correct weight is one that is challenging but still allows you to perform all the stated reps.

Keep your core muscles tight
Before any heavy lift or dynamic movement, you should tighten your core muscles to protect your lower back from injury. Imagine that someone is going to punch you in the

Exercise is most effective in small, regular bursts

stomach and brace your abs. Now hold it like that for the duration of the lift.

Always keep breathing
Never hold your breath during a lift. The general rule is to breathe in as you lower the weight, and breathe out through pursed lips as you lift.

Make it regular
How often you work out is up to you, but for best results try to train between three and five times a week. Exercise is most effective when done in small, regular bursts. Don't be tempted to train every day.

Get your rest
Your body doesn't get stronger during a workout – it gets stronger while it recovers after a workout. That's why you need to give yourself plenty of rest time between sessions and aim to get a good kip every night.

Make your workouts progressive
Aim to increase the resistance you use for an exercise by around

MINUTE
WORKOUT

10% every three or four weeks, or try to improve on the number of reps you perform in a particular time. You can't get fitter by doing the same workout with the same weight every time.

Drink more

Keep a water bottle handy and drink regularly. Dehydration will affect your performance and your workout won't be as effective.

Always eat after your workout

The 40 minutes immediately after you finish your last

rep is a vital time to get muscle-replenishing nutrients. A snack that mixes fast-acting carbs and protein (for example a bagel with cream cheese) is best.

Keep your body guessing

Your body adapts to stresses placed upon it. So if you always do the same workout your body will adapt to it and stop

growing new muscle. Keep altering your workout every few weeks to keep your body responding by building muscle and burning fat.

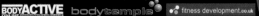

12 MINUTE WORKOUT

THE WORKOUTS

Weight-free

Core values

This workout is a great way to develop the muscles of your core – the ones around your abdomen and lower back. These muscles not only provide the much-valued six-pack, but are vital in maintaining good posture, preventing back pain and improving all areas of athletic ability.

A strong core provides the foundation upon which all other muscle gains are made, so don't move onto the more dynamic workouts until you have spent some time strengthening your core.

TARGET	LEVEL	KIT

How to do it

- ☐ Perform 10 reps of exercise 1A.
- ☐ Move immediately onto exercise 1B and do 10 reps.
- ☐ Rest for 30 seconds and then repeat exercises 1A and 1B.
- ☐ Rest for 60 seconds and then begin exercise 2A, followed immediately by 2B.
- ☐ Repeat the rest pattern as before, until you have performed 12 exercises in all.

Tips

- ☐ Keep your movements slow and controlled.
- ☐ To engage your core muscles, tense your stomach as though you were about to take a punch to the gut.
- ☐ Try to keep your back straight during each exercise.

Superset 1

1a **Split deadlift to rear flye**
10 reps (alternating feet with each rep)

Form guide: p88

1b **Dorsal raise with shoulder rotation**
10 reps (hold the raised position for two seconds)

Form guide: p92

FIT NOTE A superset is two exercises done back

DO THIS
■ 2 supersets for each group
■ Rest 30 secs between supersets
■ Rest 60 secs between groups

Superset 2

2a **Side lunge woodchop**
10 reps (5 reps each side)

Form guide: p83

2b **Side bridge**
10 reps (5 reps each side)

Form guide: p121

Superset 3

3a

Lunge with rotation
10 reps
(alternate sides with each rep)

Form guide: p81

3b **Glute bridge**
10 reps

Form guide: p120

to-back with no rest in between

Starters for ten

When time is short and all you want is a quick, simple workout that you can do anywhere, and that will hit all parts of your body, plus torch up to 200 calories in just a few minutes, then this is a great place to start.

Even if you're new to exercise, you can alter the tempo or number of reps to make this routine fit your needs.

TARGET	LEVEL	KIT
🧍🧍	1	None

How to do it

- ☐ Perform 10 reps of exercise 1A.
- ☐ Move immediately onto exercise 1B and do 10 reps.
- ☐ Rest for 60 seconds and then repeat exercises 1A and 1B.
- ☐ Rest for 90 seconds and then begin exercise 2A, doing as many reps as you can in one minute
- ☐ Move immediately onto 2B and do ten reps, then rest 60 seconds before repeating the superset.
- ☐ Repeat the pattern for superset 3.

Tips

- ☐ A wall clock with a second hand is easier than a watch for timing your one-minute sets.
- ☐ Try to pick the best tempo for you – as fast as you can manage without having to stop during each set.
- ☐ Use your full range of motion for each exercise, especially squats and press ups.

Superset 1

1a Prisoner squat
10 reps

Form guide: p74

1b Press-up
10 reps (or max you can do before failure)

Form guide: p100

FIT NOTE 'Failure' is the point at which you can ɪ

DO THIS
- 2 supersets for each group
- Rest 60 secs between supersets
- Rest 90 secs between groups

12 MINUTE WORKOUT

Superset 2

2a Jumping jacks
1 minute

Form guide: p107

2b Turkish get-up
10 reps (alternating sides each rep)

Form guide: p122

Superset 3

3a Side lunge to touch
10 reps (alternating sides each rep)

Form guide: p83

3b Jumping jacks
1 minute

Form guide: p107

onger perform an exercise with perfect form

WORKOUT
3 | Weight-free

Free for all

Just because a workout uses no equipment and only takes 12 minutes doesn't mean it can't be demanding.

This kit-free workout will test the muscles of your legs, chest, arms and abs, as well as getting your heart pumping. The result is that your metabolism will shoot up, giving you a strong fat-burning effect that lasts long after you've finished the session.

This workout is done in the form of a circuit, so you'll move from one exercise to the next with no rest in between.

TARGET	LEVEL	KIT

How to do it

- Perform each exercise in order, taking no rest between exercises.
- Do either the number of reps stated, or as many reps as you can in the time stated.
- Once you have completed one full circuit, rest for one minute before starting all over again.
- Do three circuits in total.

Tips

- Pace yourself so you can complete all your circuits.
- On the one-leg squats, keep your movements slow and controlled.
- Don't compromise form in favour of speed.

1 **Squat thrust**
30 seconds

START

Form guide: p107

6 **Jumping lunge**
30 seconds (alternating sides)

FINISH

Form guide: p82

FIT NOTE This circuit can be made tougher by

12
MINUTE
WORKOUT

2 One-leg squat (left leg)
10 reps

3 T press-up
30 seconds (alternating sides each rep)

Form guide: p74

Form guide: p103

5 Bicycles
30 seconds

4 One-leg squat (right leg)
10 reps

Form guide: p117

Form guide: p74

adding light dumb-bells

Middle manager

This session focusses on your core – those muscles around your middle – but is a step up from Workout 1. It also targets your glutes and hip flexors, which provide power and stability when running.

Your core is the connection between your lower and upper body, and almost every sport demands a strong midsection to allow for powerful all-body movements. Once you get good at this circuit, you will find that your performance in all physical activities improves as a result (a hard set of abs is just a pleasant side-effect).

TARGET	LEVEL	KIT
	2	

How to do it

☐ Perform each exercise in order, taking no rest between exercises.
☐ Do either the number of reps stated, or as many reps as you can in the time stated.
☐ Once you have completed one full circuit, rest for one minute before starting over again.
☐ Do two circuits in total.

Tips

☐ For the majority of exercises, take up to three seconds for each rep – slow is good for core training.
☐ For planks and bridges, aim to keep your body in a straight line – don't overextend your lower back.

START

1

Inch worm
30 seconds

Form guide: p124

FINISH

7 **Plank**
1 minute

Form guide: p118

FIT NOTE Your six-pack is actually one muscle –

2 Bicycles
30 seconds

Form guide: p117

3 One-leg offset touch
10 reps each leg

Form guide: p89

DO THIS

- 2 circuits
- Rest 60 secs between circuits

4 Glute bridge with leg raise
20 reps (alternating sides each rep)

Form guide: p120

6 Side bridge
10 reps each side

Form guide: p121

5 Dorsal raise with shoulder rotation
10 reps

Form guide: p92

the rectus abdominis – which runs from your ribs to your pubic bone

Half-time blast

Who says a decent workout has to eat into your precious time? This circuit will help you build stability, increase muscle mass and burn fat – and you can do it at home during the half-time interval when watching the football on telly.

The trick to making the workout effective is to keep a steady tempo for each exercise – approximately three seconds per rep – and really focus on making each movement as controlled and deliberate as possible.

TARGET	LEVEL	KIT
	2	

How to do it

- ☐ Perform each exercise in order, taking no rest between exercises.
- ☐ Take around three seconds for each rep (except squat thrusts, which should be done at speed).
- ☐ Once you have completed one full circuit, rest for one minute before starting all over again.
- ☐ Do three circuits in total.

Tips

- ☐ Make a space big enough so you can lunge in all directions on Exercise 1.
- ☐ Use your full range of motion for all exercises.
- ☐ Engage your core muscles to control all the movements.

1 Clock lunge
2 reps (1 rep = 10 lunges around the clock)

START

Form guide: p84

6 Glute bridge with leg raise
10 reps (alternating sides each rep)

FINISH

Form guide: p120

FIT NOTE Watch your breathing – out on the

12 MINUTE WORKOUT

2 **Press-up**
10 reps

3 **Lower-body rotation**
10 reps (alternating sides each rep)

Form guide: p100

Form guide: p110

5 **Squat thrust**
30 secs

4 **Prisoner squat**
10 reps

Form guide: p107

Form guide: p74

exertion phase of each rep, in on the recovery phase

Push, pull, punch

Welcome to the first of the Level 3 workouts in this guide. A pull-up bar is one of the best bits of home training equipment you can buy, and the cheap ones that fit into a doorway are as effective as any.

Pull-ups use a huge number of muscles and also target areas such as the back and biceps that are hard to train without any equipment.

Nearly all the exercises in this circuit are compound moves that take a lot of energy to perform, and many of them (squat jumps, plyo press-ups, boxing) require dynamic effort as well. In short, this will take your muscular and cardiovascular systems to their limits. Have fun!

TARGET	LEVEL	KIT
	3	

How to do it

☐ Perform each exercise in order, taking no rest between exercises.
☐ Once you have completed one full circuit, rest for one minute before starting all over again.
☐ Do four circuits in total.

Tips:

☐ Do the exercises quickly and dynamically – but always under control.
☐ Engage your core muscles to protect your lower back during dynamic movements.
☐ Mix up the shadow boxing moves as much as possible.

1 **Squat jump**
10 reps

START

Form guide: p74

5 **Shadow boxing**
1 minute

FINISH

Form guide: p106

FIT NOTE A compound movement is one that

12 MINUTE WORKOUT

2 Pull-up
10 reps
(or max you
can do)

3 Hanging knee raise
10 reps (or max you can do)

Form guide: p94

4 Plyo offset press-up
10 reps (or max you can do)

Form guide: p116

Form guide: p103

uses several muscle groups at once to bend and flex multiple joints

Elastic fantastic

This Level 1 workout won't tax you if you are already fit. But that doesn't mean it's just for beginners.

The main purpose of the workout is to improve the strength of small stabilising muscles and tendons – especially in your shoulders, knees, ankles and core – which provide the platform upon which the bigger 'glory' muscles can be built without risking injury.

Everyone should do a workout like this regularly to keep the stabilisers strong.

TARGET	LEVEL	KIT

How to do it

☐ Perform exercise 1A, followed immediately by exercise 1B.
☐ Rest for 30 seconds and then repeat superset 1 (exercises 1A and 1B) but swapping sides (use your right hand if you used the left before).
☐ Rest for 60 seconds and then begin exercise 2A, followed immediately by 2B.
☐ Repeat the pattern for superset 3.

Tips

☐ The rotator cuff muscles of the shoulder are easily injured, so keep the resistance light at first.
☐ Attach the stretch band to a solid object that won't shift or break.
☐ Manoeuvre yourself so there is tension on the band at the beginning of each move.
☐ To increase resistance, simply make the band shorter.

Superset 1

1a Internal rotation
15 reps

Form guide: p98

1b External rotation
15 reps

Form guide: p98

FIT NOTE The resistance of a stretch band

DO THIS
- 2 supersets for each group
- Rest 30 secs between supersets
- Rest 60 secs between groups

12 MINUTE WORKOUT

Superset 2

2a Split squat to one arm row
12 reps

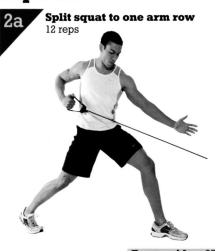

Form guide: p85

2b Split squat to one arm press
12 reps

Form guide: p85

Superset 3

3a Squat to high pull
12 reps

Form guide: p76

3b Judo throw
12 reps

Form guide: p113

increases towards the end a move, which gives a different training effect to dumb-bells

Band on the run

The stretch band is a great piece of home workout kit because it takes up virtually no space and provides an almost unlimited number of possible exercise options. If you're a gym-goer, this circuit is a great way to avoid the queues for equipment when it gets busy. You'll have finished your workout and be out the door by the time others are just getting started.

Just find something solid to attach the band to at ankle-height, and away you go.

TARGET	LEVEL	KIT
2		

How to do it

☐ Perform each exercise in order, taking no rest between exercises.
☐ Once you have completed one full circuit, rest for 45 seconds before starting all over again.
☐ Do three circuits in total.

Tips

☐ Use a clock with a second hand to time each exercise – you won't be able to look at a watch on your wrist.
☐ To increase resistance, anchor the band nearer to its middle.
☐ For complex moves such as woodchops, practise with a light resistance first to learn the move.

1
Prone stretch band pull (right hand)
30 seconds

START

Form guide: p121

FINISH

7
Split squat to one-arm press (right hand)
30 seconds

Form guide: p85

FIT NOTE If you train in a gym, this circuit can be

2

Woodchop (left to right)
30 seconds

Form guide: p112

DO THIS

- 3 circuits
- Rest 45 secs between circuits

3 **Prone stretch band pull (left hand)**
30 seconds

Form guide: p121

4

Woodchop (right to left)
30 seconds

Form guide: p112

6

Squat to high pull
30 seconds

Form guide: p76

5

Split squat to one-arm press (left hand)
30 seconds

Form guide: p85

erformed using a cable machine set to ankle-height

Planes and trains

Physical fitness isn't simply about lifting and lowering the heaviest weights possible – it's about teaching your body to be a more efficient machine. To do that you need to train it in multiple planes, using different muscle groups simultaneously, all while maintaining good posture and balance.

That's what this workout is all about. Keep the weights light, because the main thing is to perform each move perfectly. The result will be stronger joints and stabilising muscles.

TARGET	LEVEL	KIT
	1	3-6kg each

How to do it

- ☐ Perform each exercise in order, taking no rest between exercises.
- ☐ Take approximately 4 seconds per rep on each exercise.
- ☐ Once you have completed one full circuit, rest for 30 seconds before starting all over again.
- ☐ Each exercise is 'one-sided'. Choose either the left or right side for the first circuit, then swap to the other side for the following circuit.
- ☐ Do four circuits in total.

Tips

- ☐ Start on your weaker side first. You'll have more energy to perform the reps.
- ☐ Go slow and focus on balance. If you wobble or stumble, take a moment to compose yourself and start again.
- ☐ No egos! Use a light weight and get the form spot-on.

1 **Single-leg deadlift to row**
10 reps

START

Form guide: p89

4 **Side plank with lateral raise**
10 reps

FINISH

Form guide: p121

FIT NOTE Not got dumb-bells at home? Plastic

12 MINUTE WORKOUT

DO THIS

■ 4 circuits
■ Rest 30 secs between circuits

2 **One-leg curl to press**
10 reps

Form guide: p97

3 **Lunge with rotation**
10 reps alternating

Form guide: p81

milk cartons filled with water are a good substitute

Push and punch

Dumb-bells are perhaps the most versatile bit of exercise equipment you can own. For less than £30 you can buy an adjustable set that will give you thousands of options for training at home. The only downside is having to change the weights every time you change exercise.

Not with this workout. Just pick one weight and then go for it. You'll test the majority of muscles in your body and get your heart pumping as well.

If you're new to training, use a light weight and build up over time as you get fitter.

TARGET	LEVEL	KIT
🧍🧍	**1**	🏋️
		4-6kg each

How to do it

☐ Perform exercise 1A, followed immediately by exercise 1B.
☐ Rest for 30 seconds and then repeat superset 1 (exercises 1A and 1B).
☐ Rest for 60 seconds and then begin exercise 2A, followed immediately by 2B.
☐ Repeat the pattern for superset 3.

Tips

☐ Keep your core muscles engaged and maintain good posture throughout.
☐ On the timed exercises (hill climbers and jabs) go as fast as you can without losing form.

Superset 1

1a **Squat to curl to press**
10 reps

Form guide: p77

1b

Russian twist
15 reps (twisting to both sides is one rep)

Form guide: p108

FIT NOTE This session can be performed with

DO THIS
- 2 supersets for each group
- Rest 30 secs between supersets
- Rest 60 secs between groups

12
MINUTE
WORKOUT

Superset 2

2a **Hill climbers**
30 seconds

Form guide: p107

2b **Lateral raise**
10 reps

Form guide: p98

Superset 3

3a **Lunge**
10 reps
(alternating
sides each
rep)

Form guide: p78

3b **Jabs**
30 seconds

Form guide: p106

no weights at all and still give a good conditioning workout

Hot metal

With a light set of dumb-bells, this session is a great heart-pumper for newcomers to circuit training. With a heavier set of dumb-bells, this becomes a lung-busting, muscle-blasting workout for even seasoned gym-goers.

The circuit combines upper- and lower-body moves simultaneously, which requires your heart to work hard, supplying blood to many different muscles. You'll feel fitter, stronger and more coordinated – not bad for 12 minutes.

TARGET	LEVEL	KIT
🧍🧍	**1-2**	⚙️ 3-8kg each

How to do it

☐ Perform each exercise in order, taking no rest between exercises.
☐ Once you have completed one full circuit, rest for one minute before starting all over again.
☐ Do three circuits in total.

Tips

☐ Keep a steady pace for each exercise – don't compromise form for speed.
☐ Aim for 3-4 seconds for each rep.
☐ Use your full range of motion for exercises – no skimping on the squats or lunges.

1 **Squat to biceps curl**
10 reps

START

Form guide: p77

5 **Dumb-bell side lunge to touch**
10 reps (alternating sides each rep)

FINISH

Form guide: p83

FIT NOTE For squats and lunges, aim to keep

12 MINUTE WORKOUT

2

Split Romanian deadlift to rear flye
10 reps (alternating sides each rep)

Form guide: p88

3

Alternating shoulder press
10 reps (alternating sides each rep)

Form guide: p97

4

Dumb-bell lunge with rotation
10 reps (alternating sides each rep)

Form guide: p81

your knees in line with your feet to prevent unnecessary strain on your knees

Ups 'n' downs

Stand up, get down, stand up, get down… this session switches between standing and lying moves, challenging your core muscles and your cardio fitness at the same time. The six exercises combine to target every muscle in your body, meaning that you can walk away after 12 minutes knowing that your training is balanced and efficient.

Your core especially will feel the burn on this one, so keep all your movements deliberate and stop if you feel your form going. Over-stressing your core is the quickest route to lower-back problems.

TARGET	LEVEL	KIT
	2	5-10kg each

How to do it

☐ Perform each exercise in order, taking no rest between exercises.
☐ Once you have completed one full circuit, rest for 90 seconds before starting all over again.
☐ Do three circuits in total.

Tips

☐ Aim for around three seconds for each rep (except jabs, where you should go as fast as possible).
☐ Be careful when moving from a lying to a standing position between exercises.
☐ Keep a straight back and tight core to avoid straining your lower back.

1 START
Lunge to curl
10 reps (alternating sides each rep)

Form guide: p80

6 FINISH
Jabs
30 seconds

Form guide: p106

FIT NOTE Aim to make the eccentric (lowering)

12 MINUTE WORKOUT

DO THIS

- 3 circuits
- Rest 90 secs between circuits

2 **Dumb-bell press up**
10 reps

3 **Russian twist**
10 reps
(both ways
equals one rep)

Form guide: p102

Form guide: p108

5 **Renegade row**
10 reps (alternating sides each rep)

4 **Squat to press**
10 reps

Form guide: p91

Form guide: p77

portion of a lift slow and controlled, and the concentric (lifting) portion fast and powerful

Combo special

Most people in a gym only train one muscle at a time. That's why it takes them so long to get through a workout!

These exercises work multiple muscle groups simultaneously, saving you valuable time and making your training sessions more efficient. Combo moves are simply different exercises stitched together to create a new exercise, and you are only limited by your imagination as to how to create these super-moves.

A perfect example is the first exercise of this session. It combines a press up, a burpee, a clean and a press to make a move that is almost a workout in itself.

TARGET	LEVEL	KIT
	2	5-10kg each

How to do it

- ☐ Perform each exercise in order, taking no rest between exercises.
- ☐ Once you have completed one full circuit, rest for one minute before starting all over again.
- ☐ Do three circuits in total.

Tips

- ☐ Make all your movements controlled and deliberate. Good form is all-important.
- ☐ Use a wall clock to time the exercises – you won't be able to keep an eye on a wrist watch.

1 **Press-up to burpee to clean to press**
10 reps

START

Form guide: p123

6 **Uppercuts**
30 seconds (alternating sides each rep)

FINISH

Form guide: p106

FIT NOTE Plyometric exercises, such as jumping

DO THIS

- 3 circuits
- Rest 60 secs between circuits

2 **Side lunge woodchop**
10 reps each side

Form guide: p113

3 **Punch up crunch**
30 seconds (alternating sides reach rep)

5 **Jumping lunge with twist**
30 seconds (alternating sides each rep)

Form guide: p116

Form guide: p82

lunges, use the most fast-twitch muscle fibres – ones that have the best potential for growth

Hell's bells

It's time to go heavy. This workout is designed to maximise muscle growth while minimising time. The exercises target the major muscle groups using compound movements, which will stimulate a big hormone surge in your body to promote new muscle.

Pick the heaviest weight you can manage for each exercise without compromising good form. You should be able to complete the reps for each set, but only just. If it feels like you could do more reps the weight is too light.

TARGET	LEVEL	KIT
	3	12-20kg each

How to do it

- ☐ Perform exercise 1A, followed immediately by exercise 1B.
- ☐ Rest for 30 seconds and then repeat superset 1 (exercises 1A and 1B).
- ☐ Rest for 90 seconds and then do exercise 2A, followed immediately by 2B.
- ☐ Rest for 30 seconds and then repeat superset 2.
- ☐ Repeat the pattern for superset 3.

Tips

- ☐ Aim to hit failure at or near the end of each set.
- ☐ Keep your ego in check – don't compromise good form for the sake of heavy weights.

Superset 1

1a Dumb-bell incline bench press
10 reps

Form guide: p105

1b Dumb-bell incline bench row
10 reps

Form guide: p91

FIT NOTE Targeting large muscle groups creates

DO THIS
- 2 supersets for each group
- Rest 30 secs between supersets
- Rest 90 secs between groups

12 MINUTE WORKOUT

Superset 2

2a Dumb-bell squat to press
10 reps

Form guide: p77

2b

Dumb-bell high pull
10 reps

Form guide: p99

Superset 3

3a Dumb-bell seated Russian twist
10 reps (both sides equals one rep)

Form guide: p111

3b Lower body rotation (straight leg)
10 reps (each side equals one rep)

Form guide: p110

a hormone surge that helps build muscle in all areas of your body

WORKOUT 15
Dumb-bells & gym ball

Steady Eddie

The gym ball is a handy piece of kit to have at home. It's a cheap alternative to a workout bench, and you can hide it under the bed when it's not in use (best to let the air out first). But the main value of the gym ball lies in its wobbliness.

Keeping the ball steady while you sit or lie on it requires you to use your core muscles for stability, which improves posture and helps to provide that all-important six-pack. Because these exercises are so unstable, start with a light weight and build up once you have mastered the movements.

TARGET	LEVEL	KIT
	2	5-10kg each

How to do it

☐ Perform each exercise in order, taking no rest between exercises.
☐ Once you have completed one full circuit, rest for 30 seconds before starting all over again.
☐ Do five circuits in total.

Tips

☐ Use your core muscles to minimise the wobble on the gym ball.
☐ When lying back on the ball keep your head and shoulders supported.
☐ Keep your body as straight as you can when lying on the ball.

1 **Gym ball alternating chest press**
16 reps (alternating sides each rep)

START

Form guide: p105

4 **Gym ball Russian twist**
10 reps (twisting both sides equals 1 rep)

FINISH

Form guide: p111

FIT NOTE The correct size of gym ball is one

12 MINUTE WORKOUT

2

Gym ball prone alternating row

16 reps (alternating sides each rep)

Form guide: p91

3

Squat to rotating shoulder press

16 reps (alternating sides each rep)

Form guide: p77

where when you lie back on it with your knees bent at 90°, your body is horizontal

Shake, rattle & roll

When the queues for the equipment build up in the gym, grab a spare gym ball, find a quiet corner and knock out this fast workout. You'll be finished while the others are still programming their treadmills.

This session won't leave you gasping for breath, but it will train your body to stabilise itself in a range of different planes. You will become functionally fitter – able to do more, more efficiently.

Even seasoned weight trainers can benefit from a day away from the heavy barbells, doing this workout, and focussing on the deep stabilising muscles.

TARGET	LEVEL	KIT
🧍🧍	1	⚫

How to do it

☐ Perform exercise 1A, followed immediately by exercise 1B.
☐ Rest for 30 seconds and then repeat superset 1 (exercises 1A and 1B).
☐ Rest for 90 seconds and then do exercise 2A, followed immediately by 2B.
☐ Rest for 30 seconds and then repeat superset 2.
☐ Repeat the pattern for superset 3.

Tips

☐ Practise moves before the workout to assess where best to place your feet on the ball.
☐ Make your moves slow and deliberate, concentrating on stabilising the ball's wobble.

Superset 1

1a   **Gym ball leg curl**
10 reps

Form guide: p126

1b   **Gym ball jackknife**
10 reps

Form guide: p126

FIT NOTE Swapping a bench for a gym ball turn

DO THIS
- 2 supersets for each group
- Rest 30 secs between supersets
- Rest 90 secs between groups

12 MINUTE WORKOUT

Superset 2

2a **Gym ball split squat with rotation**
10 reps (twist left first set, right second set)

Form guide: p82

2b **Gym ball squat and reach**
10 reps

Form guide: p75

Superset 3

3a **Gym ball twisting crunch**
10 reps

Form guide: p117

3b **Gym ball plank**
30 seconds

Form guide: p120

ny exercise into a core stability exercise

Rolling thunder

Many men don't like gym balls – there's something a bit 'girly' about them. They feel that men should use heavy things made out of iron, not rubber balls.

If that has been your opinion, this workout may just change your mind. It requires you to perform seven exercises back-to-back, testing a different part of your body with each one, but always making you work those core muscles to keep your body stable on the gym ball. Do it with strong, controlled movements and you'll get a full-body muscle burn and good cardio workout to boot.

Balls to all those guys who don't like balls.

TARGET	LEVEL	KIT
	2	

How to do it

☐ Perform each exercise in order, taking no rest between exercises.
☐ Once you have completed one full circuit, rest for one minute before starting all over again.
☐ Do three circuits in total.

Tips

☐ Note that you will need a solid wall for one exercise.
☐ Hold each exercise for a second at the point of maximum contraction. It will teach your body to control its own weight.

1
START

Gym ball twisting jackknife
12 reps (alternating sides each rep)

Form guide: p126

FINISH

7

Gym ball pistol
5 reps each leg

Form guide: p75

FIT NOTE Swap one-leg pistols for two-leg wall

2 Gym ball press-up
12 reps

Form guide: p103

3 Gym ball hip raise to leg curl
12 reps

Form guide: p126

DO THIS

- 3 circuits
- Rest 60 secs between circuits

4 Gym ball back extension
12 reps

Form guide: p92

6 Gym ball twisting crunch
12 reps (alternating sides each rep)

Form guide: p117

5 Gym ball supine reach
12 reps (alternating sides each rep)

Form guide: p93

squats if the former prove too difficult

Slam dunk

The beauty of the medicine ball is that you can slam it on the floor or throw it against the wall without taking chunks out of your décor. You can't do that with a dumb-bell.

The dynamic throwing exercises you do with a medicine ball utilise the fast-twitch muscle fibres in your body. These are the fibres that are used in explosive movements such as heavy lifts, jumps and throws (as opposed to slow-twitch fibres which come into play during endurance exercises such as running) and they have the most potential for growth.

Adding a medicine ball into your routine is a fast way to add muscle to your frame.

TARGET	LEVEL	KIT
	2	4-6kg

How to do it

☐ Perform each exercise in order, taking no rest between exercises.
☐ Once you have completed one full circuit, rest for 90 seconds before starting all over again.
☐ Do three circuits in total.

Tips

☐ Remove anything breakable from the vicinity – a wayward throw-down could be costly.
☐ Watch out for sweaty hands that could undermine your grip on the ball.
☐ Pick a weight of ball that is challenging but allows you to complete the moves without compromising good form.

1

START

Throw down
30 seconds

Form guide: p127

FINISH

7 **Russian twist**
30 seconds

Form guide: p108

FIT NOTE If maintaining grip proves tricky, use

2 Squat and reach
30 seconds

Form guide: p75

3 Medicine ball press-up
30 seconds

Form guide: p102

4 Lunge chop (to left)
30 seconds

Form guide: p113

6 Lunge chop (to right)
30 seconds

Form guide: p113

5 Crunch throw
30 seconds

Form guide: p116

a medicine ball with handles

Take your medicine

There are only three exercises in this circuit. Just three. What could be easier?

Don't be fooled, this is a heart-pumping, muscle-burning workout that will keep gym masochists happy when time is short. The opening exercise is really a combination of three exercises – press up, burpee and overhead squat – with a heavy ball thrown in to make it more interesting. It takes coordination, muscle stability, core strength and flexibility to perform this exercise with fluidity, so practise it first with no weight before you begin the circuit.

TARGET	LEVEL	KIT
	3	4–6kg

How to do it

- ☐ Perform each exercise in order, taking no rest between exercises.
- ☐ Once you have completed one full circuit, rest for 30 seconds before starting all over again.
- ☐ Do four circuits in total.

Tips

- ☐ Practise all moves first before adding in the medicine ball.
- ☐ Maintain a pace that is challenging, but that allows you to complete all your reps without having to stop.
- ☐ Engage your core muscles to protect your lower spine during each exercise.

1

Medicine ball press up to burpee to overhead squat
10 reps

START

Form guide: p123

2

Medicine ball sledgehammer
15 reps

FINISH

Form guide: p127

FIT NOTE If you find that you lean forward too

DO THIS
- 4 circuits
- Rest 30 secs between circuits

3

Medicine ball seated Russian twist
10 reps (both ways equals one rep)

Form guide: p111

far on the overhead squats, spend more time stretching your hamstrings and hip flexors

All bar none

The barbell is the close cousin of the dumb-bell. The main difference is that a barbell is more stable to handle than a dumb-bell, allowing you to perform similar exercises with more weight. More weight equals more muscle.

With this workout you'll do a series of classic compound barbell moves – but all linked together to form a complex circuit. Three sets of ten reps of seven exercises would take most gym-goers up to an hour to complete. You'll be done and dusted in 12 minutes, having worked every muscle in your body and boosted your fat-burning metabolism to boot.

TARGET	LEVEL	KIT
	2	10-25kg

How to do it

☐ Use the same weight of barbell for each exercise.
☐ Perform each exercise in order, taking no rest between exercises.
☐ Once you have completed one full circuit, rest for 1 minute before starting all over again.
☐ Do three circuits in total.

Tips

☐ Don't put the bar down during the circuit – it is designed so you can move from one exercise to the next without a break.
☐ Pick a weight that is challenging but allows you to complete all your reps without stopping.
☐ Use collars on an Olympic bar to prevent the plates slipping.

1

START

Romanian deadlift
10 reps

Form guide: p86

FINISH

7

Barbell biceps curl
10 reps

Form guide: p125

FIT NOTE A standard Olympic barbell weighs

12 MINUTE WORKOUT

2 Bent over row
10 reps

Form guide: p90

3 Barbell squat
10 reps

Form guide: p72

DO THIS

- 3 circuits
- Rest 60 secs between circuits

4 Shoulder press
10 reps

Form guide: p96

6 Barbell rotation
10 reps (alternating sides each rep)

Form guide: p110

5 Lunge
10 reps (alternating sides each rep)

Form guide: p80

20kg before you add any weight plates

Heavy duty

It's time to go heavy. Doing compound moves with a heavy barbell will stimulate a surge of testosterone which is vital to build muscle.

In order to save time you will still do exercises back-to-back in the form of a circuit, but only three of them with eight reps each. Pick the heaviest weight you can manage, but don't compromise on form – it's better to pick a manageable weight and get each move right than to lift heavy weights badly.

TARGET	LEVEL	KIT
	3	30-40kg

How to do it

☐ Use the same weight of barbell for each exercise.
☐ Perform each exercise in order, taking no rest between exercises.
☐ Once you have completed one full circuit, rest for 60 seconds before starting again.
☐ Do five circuits in total.

Tips

☐ The power clean to front squat should be performed as one fluid motion. If it proves too tricky, spilt the exercise into distinct parts.
☐ Aim to hit failure on each exercise at or near the rep range.
☐ Try to regulate your breathing with the movements of each rep – out on the exertion phase, in on the recovery phase.

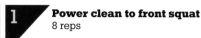

1 **Power clean to front squat**
8 reps

START

Form guide: p76

FIT NOTE A rep range in the region of 8-12 per

2 **Push press**
8 reps

3 **Romanian deadlift to bent over row**
8 reps

FINISH

Form guide: p97

Form guide: p88

set is considered the optimum for building muscle

Barbell & bench

Push me, pull you

There are four main movements in weight training: push, pull, squat, bend. Any balanced all-body muscle-building workout should be based around these four moves.

Too often men will focus on the exercises they like best, or the muscles they want to build most – that's why you see far more people in gyms doing bench presses than you see doing rows. But if you target your chest without doing the equivalent work on your back, you risk postural problems.

This workout will hit the muscles of your body equally by pairing exercises that are the opposites of each other.

TARGET	LEVEL	KIT
	3	

How to do it

☐ Perform exercise 1A, followed immediately by exercise 1B.
☐ Rest for 30 seconds and then repeat superset 1 (exercises 1A and 1B).
☐ Rest for 90 seconds and then do exercise 2A, followed immediately by 2B.
☐ Rest for 30 seconds and then repeat superset 2.
☐ Repeat the pattern for superset 3.

Tips

☐ For each exercise, choose the heaviest weight that still allows you to complete all the reps.
☐ Use a spotter (see note below, right) on exercises such as the bench press and squat if you are training at maximal effort.

Superset 1

1a **Power clean**
10 reps

Form guide: p76

1b

Pull up
10 reps

Form guide: p94

FIT NOTE A spotter is someone who can help

DO THIS

- 2 supersets for each group
- Rest 30 secs between supersets
- Rest 90 secs between groups

12 MINUTE WORKOUT

Superset 2

2a **Bench press**
10 reps

Form guide: p104

2b **Bent over row**
10 reps

Form guide: p90

Superset 3

3a **Squat**
10 reps

Form guide: p72

3b

Push press
10 reps

Form guide: p97

take the weight of the bar during an exercise if you hit exhaustion and can't control the bar

Get your back up

The final five workouts in this guide will focus on training specific parts of the body. If you prefer to organise your training regime by body-part splits, then there's a 12 minute workout to suit you.

This session pairs exercises that target the back and biceps. These two muscle groups are often trained together because they frequently work as a team on pulling movements such as rows and pull-ups.

TARGET	LEVEL	KIT
🧍🧍	**2**	🏋️

How to do it

☐ Perform exercise 1A, followed immediately by exercise 1B.
☐ Rest for 45 seconds and then repeat superset 1 (exercises 1A and 1B).
☐ Rest for another 45 seconds and then repeat superset 1 again.
☐ Rest for one minute and then do exercise 2A, followed immediately by 2B.
☐ Repeat superset 2 twice more, resting 45 seconds between supersets.

Tips

☐ For back exercises, contract your shoulder blades to stabilise your shoulders and scapulae before your start.
☐ At the point of maximum contraction, squeeze the muscle as hard as you can to enhance the muscle-growth effect.

Superset 1

1a

Chin-up
Max reps

Form guide: p95

1b
Bent over row
12 reps

Form guide: p90

FIT NOTE 'Splits' is a term to describe how you

DO THIS
- 3 supersets for each group
- Rest 45 secs between supersets
- Rest 60 secs between groups

12 MINUTE WORKOUT

Superset 2

2a   Incline bench dumb-bell reverse flye
12 reps

Form guide: p93

2b   Incline bench dumb-bell biceps curl
12 reps

Form guide: p125

break up your training regime. Many men will split their weekly regime by body part

24 | Chest & triceps

Leader of the pec

If the previous workout was all about pulling, this one is all about pushing.

Your chest muscles (pectorals) and triceps (the rear portion of your upper arm) both come into play whenever you push something away from you. This movement manifests itself most obviously in that classic weight training exercise, the bench press.

This workout moves from stability exercise, to compound exercise to isolation exercises to give your chest and triceps the maximum possible growth stimulus in the minimum possible time.

TARGET	LEVEL	KIT
	2	

How to do it

☐ Perform one set of exercise 1, doing as many as you can comfortably manage, but no more than 20.
☐ Rest for one minute, then perform exercise 2.
☐ Do four sets in total of exercise 2, resting one minute between each.
☐ Rest for another minute and move on to exercise 3A, followed immediately by 3B.
☐ Rest for one more minute before repeating superset 3 (3A and 3B).

Tips

☐ For the bench press, pick a weight that you can manage eight times, but no more than 12.
☐ If possible, use a spotter for the bench press.
☐ Make each movement slow and controlled, taking 3-4 seconds for each rep.

1 **Medicine ball passing press-up**
1 set, 10-20 reps

Form guide: p102

FIT NOTE When performing bench presses,

DO THIS

- Exercise 1: 1 set, 10-20 reps
- Exercise 2: 4 sets, 8-12 reps
- Superset 3: 2 supersets, 12 reps

12 MINUTE WORKOUT

2 **Bench press**
4 sets, 8-12 reps

Superset 3

3a **Dumb-bell bench flye**
12 reps

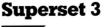

Form guide: p105

3b **Dumb-bell lying triceps press**
12 reps

Form guide: p104

Form guide: p125

retract your shoulder blades to stabilise your shoulder joints and place the focus on your chest

Ab-solution

Washboard stomach, abs, six-pack… call it what you like, but the Holy Grail of all serious weight trainers is a solid, visible set of abdominals. Strange, then, that so many people are unaware of the best way to train them.

Like other muscles, abdominals respond best to reps in the 8-12 range, with the final rep being to failure. In order to achieve this you need to add resistance to your crunches, which is exactly what you'll do in this workout.

You'll start by attacking your abs, and their supporting muscles, from several different angles, and then take the abdominals to exhaustion using three sets of weighted crunches.

TARGET	LEVEL	KIT
	2	

How to do it

☐ Perform exercises 1 to 4 in order with no rest in between, to make one giant set.
☐ Do three giant sets in total, resting one minute between each.
☐ Rest for another minute and then move on to the final exercise, the weighted crunch.
☐ Do three sets of weighted crunches in total, resting one minute between each set.

Tips

☐ For the first two exercises make your movements dynamic but controlled. Use your abs to decelerate the motion of the ball.
☐ Take at least four seconds for each weighted crunch, making the lowering part as controlled as possible.

Giant set 1

1a

Medicine ball sledgehammer
15 reps

Form guide: p127

1c **Bicycles**
15 reps (both sides equals one rep)

Form guide: p117

FIT NOTE The strongest abs in the world still

12 MINUTE WORKOUT

**Medicine ball
Russian twist**
15 reps (both sides
equals one rep)

Form guide: p109

1d Aquaman
15 reps (both sides equals one rep)

Weighted crunch
8-10 reps

Form guide: p92

Form guide: p114

won't show if they are covered with fat. Aim to reduce your body fat with good diet

26 | Shoulders & traps

Delt force

Delts and traps – that's muscle-speak for your shoulders and upper back. To give them their full names, the deltoids are the muscles that surround your shoulder joint, and the trapezius is the large diamond-shaped muscle beneath your neck that comes into play whenever you shrug your shoulders.

This workout starts with a rotator cuff (the stabiliser muscles in your shoulder) warm-up, followed by supersets of heavy compound moves and lighter, more targeted exercises to take the muscle groups to full exhaustion.

TARGET	LEVEL	KIT
🧍🧍	**2**	🏋️

How to do it

☐ Perform exercise 1, doing 30 seconds on each arm, and then rest for one minute.
☐ Do exercise 2A, followed immediately by exercise 2B with no rest in between.
☐ Rest for one minute then repeat superset 2 (2A and 2B) another two times, resting for 60 seconds between supersets.
☐ Rest for another minute and then do three sets of superset 3 (3A and 3B), resting for 60 seconds between supersets.

Tips

☐ For the prone pulls use a light resistance. The idea is to warm up the rotator cuff without over-stressing it.
☐ Only lift the weights to shoulder-height on the lateral raises.

1

Prone stretch band pull
30 seconds each arm

Form guide: p121

FIT NOTE No gym membership? Most of these

DO THIS
- 1 set of exercise 1
- 3 sets of superset 2
- 3 sets of superset 3
- 1 minute rest between each

12 MINUTE WORKOUT

Superset 2

2a

Barbell push press
8-10 reps

Form guide: p97

2b **Lateral raise**
10-12 reps

Form guide: p98

Superset 3

3a **Barbell shrug**
8-10 reps

Form guide: p99

3b

Dumb-bell high pull
10-12 reps

Form guide: p99

exercises can be performed using a single item of kit, such as stretch band or dumb-bells

Two legs good

Poor old legs. They carry you around all day, but when it comes to training they often get ignored in favour of the 'glory' upper body muscles.

This is a mistake, not only because it leads to an unbalanced physique, but because leg training is one of the best ways to get a more muscular upper body. When you lift weights, you release hormones that encourage new muscle growth all over your body. The bigger the muscles trained, the bigger the hormonal surge, and muscles don't come much bigger than the ones in your legs.

TARGET	LEVEL	KIT
	2-3	

How to do it

☐ Perform exercise 1, the clock lunge. Once round the clock takes ten lunges, so a circuit in each direction takes 20 lunges.
☐ Rest for 30 seconds, then perform exercise 2.
☐ Rest for another 30 seconds, then perform exercise 2 again.
☐ Repeat the pattern for the remaining exercises, doing two sets of each with 30 seconds rest in between.

Tips

☐ For squats and lunges use the biggest range of motion you can manage without compromising good form.
☐ On most heavy lifts, take three seconds for the eccentric (lowering) portion, and then perform the concentric (lifting) portion quickly and powerfuly.

1 Clock lunge
20 reps (once round the clock in each direction)

Form guide: p84

4 Squat jump
10 reps

Form guide: p74

FIT NOTE The glutes – gluteus maximus – are

DO THIS

- Exercise 1, once round the clock in each direction (20 lunges in total)
- 2 sets each of remaining exercises
- 30 seconds rest between each

12 MINUTE WORKOUT

2 Barbell squat
8-10 reps

Form guide: p72

3 Barbell Romanian deadlift
8-10 reps

Form guide: p86

5 Gym ball hip raise to leg curl
10 reps

Form guide: p126

6

Calf raise
10 reps each leg

Form guide: p124

the largest muscles in your body

12 MINUTE WORKOUT

FORM GUIDES

MINUTE WORKOUT

FORM GUIDES

BARBELL SQUAT

A classic power move, the squat builds muscle all over your body. Make it the cornerstone of your training.

◢ Head up, looking forward.

◢ Shoulders and elbows back.

◢ Rest the bar on the back of your shoulders, not your neck.

◢ Brace your core muscles by holding your abdominals tight.

◢ Feet just wider than shoulder-width apart, with toes turned out slightly.

12 MINUTE WORKOUT

◢ Keep your head up and looking forward.

◢ Keep your torso as upright as you can manage.

◢ Maintain the natural arch in your back – don't allow your spine to curve forwards.

◢ Bend at the knees and lower your backside towards the floor as far as you can manage.

◢ Knees in line with feet.

◢ Push back up through your heels.

FORM GUIDES

PRISONER SQUAT

◢ Follow the same form guides as for the barbell squat on the previous page.

◢ Touch your fingers to your temples and keep your elbows back.

◢ Keep your back upright and knees in line with your feet.

◢ Squat as low as you can manage without losing form.

SQUAT JUMP

◢ Lower into a deep squat with your arms by your sides.

◢ Pause briefly and engage your core muscles.

◢ Spring up powerfully.

◢ As you land, bend your knees to absorb the impact and go straight into the next squat.

ONE-LEG SQUAT

◢ Keep your back straight with your shoulders back and core muscles engaged to hold your body steady.

◢ Hold your arms out for balance.

◢ Lower slowly as far as you can manage before pushing back up.

◢ Keep your bending your knee in line with your foot.

GYM BALL PISTOL

◢ Place a gym ball between your lower back and a wall.

◢ Put your standing foot slightly in front of your body.

◢ Bend your knee in line with your foot, and slowly lower as far as you can.

◢ Hold your raised leg out in front of you as you roll down the ball.

MEDICINE BALL SQUAT AND REACH

◢ Stand up straight, holding a medicine ball to your chest.

◢ Feet just wider than shoulder-width apart with toes turned out slightly.

◢ As you squat down, press the ball away from you at chest-height.

◢ The counterbalance of the ball should allow you to squat lower than usual.

ALSO TRY

GYM BALL SQUAT AND REACH

FORM GUIDES

SQUAT TO HIGH PULL

◢ Attach the centre of a stretch band to a solid object at floor level.

◢ Get tension on the band before squatting down facing the band.

◢ As you stand up, pull the handles up to shoulder-height, leading with your elbows.

◢ Keep your back straight and core braced throughout.

POWER CLEAN TO FRONT SQUAT

◢ Start in a deadlift position (see p87 for more tips), with the bar close to your shins and directly beneath your shoulders.

◢ Grip the bar just outside your legs and keep your back straight and core braced as you drop your hips to begin the lift.

◢ Pull the bar up powerfully in front of you, keeping the bar close to your body and raising your elbows high.

◢ As the bar reaches chest-height, flip it over so it rests on your fingers and the fronts of your shoulders.

◢ With your elbows pointing forward and your back as upright as you can manage, lower into a squat, keeping your knees in line with your feet.

◢ Push back up and then carefully reset the bar on the floor to begin the next rep.

SQUAT TO BICEPS CURL

◢ Hold dumb-bells at your sides with palms facing in.

◢ Lower into a squat. As you stand, curl the weights to your chest, turning your palms so they face up.

◢ Keep your elbows tucked into your sides as you curl the dumb-bells.

SQUAT TO CURL TO PRESS

After curling the dumb-bells to your chest, press them overhead, turning your palms to face forward.

SQUAT TO PRESS

◢ Hold dumb-bells at shoulder-height with your elbows out to the sides.

◢ Lower into a squat with a straight back and knees in line with your feet.

◢ As you stand up, press the weights directly overhead.

◢ Lower the weights as you drop into the next squat.

SQUAT TO ROTATING SHOULDER PRESS

◢ Hold dumb-bells at shoulder-height with your elbows out to the sides.

◢ As you stand up, rotate your body to one side, rising up on your toes.

◢ At the same time, press one of the weights up and across your body.

◢ Return to the start and press to the other side on the next rep.

FORM GUIDES

LUNGE

Lunging works all your lower body muscles and improves stability and sporting performance.

◢ Head up, looking forward.

◢ Body upright with core muscles engaged.

◢ Hold weights by your sides with palms facing in.

◢ Feet apart slightly with toes pointing forward.

12 MINUTE WORKOUT

Shoulders back – don't be tempted to hunch forward.

Keep your body upright throughout the exercise.

Take a big step forward, keeping both feet pointing forward.

Bend your leading leg until your thigh is parallel to the floor.

Lower your rear knee until it almost touches the floor.

Don't let your leading knee travel past your toes.

Return to the start by pushing off your front foot.

FORM GUIDES

BARBELL LUNGE

◢ The form points are the same as for the lunge on the previous page.

◢ Hold a barbell across the back of your shoulders, not your neck.

◢ Pull your elbows and shoulders back.

◢ Keep your body upright throughout.

LUNGE TO CURL

◢ Hold dumb-bells at your sides with palms facing in.

◢ Lunge forward, keeping your feet pointing forward and your body upright.

◢ At the same time, curl the dumb-bells up to chest-height, turning your wrists so that your palms face upwards.

◢ As you curl, keep your elbows tucked into your sides.

◢ Push back to the start and lower the weights to your sides again.

12 MINUTE WORKOUT

LUNGE WITH ROTATION

◢ Step into a lunge and hold your arms out in front of you at chest-height.

◢ Keep your back upright and core braced, with feet pointing forward.

◢ At the lowest point of the lunge – with front thigh parallel to the floor – rotate your body to one side.

◢ Return to facing forward before pushing off your front foot to return to the start postiion.

◢ On the next repetition, rotate to the other side.

ALSO TRY

DUMB-BELL LUNGE WITH ROTATION

FORM GUIDES

JUMPING LUNGE

⬥ Get into a lunge position with back upright and core braced.

⬥ Jump up and swap leg positions in mid-air.

⬥ Land in lunge postion and pause for a second before pushing up for another jump. Swap leg positions again.

JUMPING LUNGE WITH TWIST

⬥ Start in a lunge position holding a dumb-bell outside your leading thigh.

⬥ Jump up and swap leg positions while bringing the weight across your body.

⬥ Land in lunge position on the other side, and repeat the jump in the other direction.

GYM BALL SPLIT SQUAT WITH ROTATION

⬥ Stand in a split stance with one foot ahead of the other, both feet pointing forward and your back upright.

⬥ Hold a gym ball in front of you at chest-height.

⬥ Lower into a lunge position while rotating your body to one side.

⬥ Alternate sides each rep.

12 MINUTE WORKOUT

SIDE LUNGE WOODCHOP

◢ Stand up straight and hold your hands together over one shoulder.

◢ Take a big step sideways, keeping both feet pointed forward, and lower onto your leading knee, keeping your training leg straight.

◢ At the same time, bring your arms down and across your body in a chopping motion, before pushing back to the start.

SIDE LUNGE TO TOUCH

◢ From standing, take a big step to the side, with both feet pointing forward.

◢ Lower onto your leading knee while keeping your trailing leg straight.

◢ With a straight back, lean forward to touch your leading foot before pushing back to the start.

◢ Alternate sides with each rep.

ALSO TRY

DUMB-BELL SIDE LUNGE TO TOUCH

CLOCK LUNGE

◢ For this exercise you lunge towards different points around the clock, until you have completed 10 lunges in total to bring you back to the beginning.

◢ The first lunge is straight ahead, leading with your right leg, the next at 45˚ to your right, then 90˚ to the right, then behind you at 45˚ to the right, then directing backwards leading with your right leg, then backwards leading with your left leg, then at 45˚ behind you to the left... and so on until your final lunge is forwards leading with your left leg.

◢ For each lunge, keep your body upright and core braced.

◢ Aim to keep your feet pointing forwards with each lunge.

SPLIT SQUAT TO ONE-ARM ROW

◢ Attach a stretch band to a solid object at floor level and hold the handle in your right hand with tension on the band.

◢ With both feet pointing in line with the band, take a split stance with left leg forward and lower your body by bending both knees until you back knee is close to the floor.

◢ Rotate your torso towards the band while keeping your body upright.

◢ As you stand up, rotate your torso away from the band and pull the handle into your side.

◢ Return slowly to the start and repeat.

SPLIT SQUAT TO ONE-ARM PRESS

◢ Attach a stretch band to a solid object at floor level and hold the handle in your right hand with tension on the band.

◢ Facing away from the band, take a split stance with your leg forward and the handle held at shoulder-height.

◢ Lower your body by bending your knees, and turn your torso towards the band while keeping your body upright.

◢ As you stand up, rotate your torso away from the band and press the handle up and away from you.

◢ Return slowly to the start and repeat.

FORM GUIDES

ROMANIAN DEADLIFT

This move targets your glutes and hamstrings as well as your core muscles.

◢ Head up and looking straight ahead.

◢ Hold your stomach muscles tight for the duration of the lift.

◢ Shoulders back and shoulder blades engaged to stabilise your upper body.

◢ Hold the bar just outside your thighs with an overhand grip.

◢ Feet shoulder-width apart with toes pointing forward.

◢ Bar resting against your thighs.

12 MINUTE WORKOUT

◢ Keep your shoulders back – don't hunch.

◢ Head up, looking forward (without over-extending your neck).

◢ Bend at the hips, keeping your back straight.

◢ Use your glute muscles to control the descent of the bar.

◢ Let the bar run down your shins.

◢ Bend your knees slightly to allow the bar to travel vertically downwards.

◢ Lower bar slowly as far as is comfortable, before pushing your hips forward to return to the start.

◢ Keep your weight distributed evenly over your feet – don't let your weight tip you forward.

ROMANIAN DEADLIFT TO BENT OVER ROW

◢ Follow the form for the Romanian deadlift on the previous page.

◢ Lower the bar down your shins by bending at the hips and unlocking your knees, while keeping your back straight.

◢ At your lowest point, pause and then pull the bar into your abdomen, squeezing your shoulder blades together.

◢ Reverse the movement to the start.

DUMB-BELL SPLIT DEADLIFT TO REAR FLYE

◢ Take a small step forward and lean over at the hips, lowering the weights down your front shin.

◢ Keep your weight on your front foot and your back straight.

◢ At the lowest point, hold the position and raise your arms out to the sides, squeezing your shoulder blades together.

ALSO TRY

SPLIT ROMANIAN DEADLIFT TO REAR FLYE

ONE-LEG OFFSET TOUCH

◢ Stand on one leg, with your back upright and toe pointing forward.

◢ Lean forward slowly at the hips, keeping your back straight.

◢ Bend your knee slightly to maintain your balance.

◢ Touch the floor to the outside of your foot and return to the start without losing your balance.

SINGLE-LEG DEADLIFT TO ROW

◢ Hold dumb-bells by your sides and keep your back straight with your core muscles engaged.

◢ Lean forward slowly at the hips with a straight back and let the weights hang straight down.

◢ Hold the position while you draw the weights into your sides. Reverse the movement back to the start.

FORM GUIDES

BENT OVER ROW

This compound move builds the muscles of your mid-back while strengthening your core.

◢ Back straight and core muscles engaged.

◢ Shoulders directly over the bar.

◢ Lean forward at the hips.

◢ Bend your knees slightly.

◢ Hold the bar just outside your shins with an overhand grip.

◢ Hold your position as you lift the bar – don't rock up and down.

◢ Squeeze your shoulder blades together.

◢ Feet just wider than shoulder-width apart with toes pointing forward.

◢ Pull the bar into your abdomen and hold for a second before lowering slowly.

12 MINUTE WORKOUT

RENEGADE ROW

◢ Get into a press-up position while holding dumb-bells at shoulder-width.

◢ Feet apart for balance.

◢ Keep your body straight from head to heels, and engage your core muscles.

◢ Draw one of the weights into your side and lower again before repeating on the other side.

GYM BALL PRONE ALTERNATING ROW

◢ Lie on a gym ball with your body straight and the ball beneath your chest.

◢ Hold dumb-bells on either side of the ball.

◢ Alternately draw one weight up while lowering the other.

◢ Keep your body steady throughout.

DUMB-BELL INCLINE BENCH ROW

◢ Set the bench at 30˚ to 45˚.

◢ Lie face-down on the bench and let the weights hang straight down with palms facing backwards.

◢ Draw the dumb-bells into your sides and squeeze your shoulder blades together before lowering slowly.

FORM GUIDES

DORSAL RAISE WITH SHOULDER ROTATION

◢ Lie face-down on a mat with your arms out to the sides, palms facing down.

◢ Lift your shoulders off the mat.

◢ At the same time twist your palms, so your thumbs point to the ceiling, and squeeze your shoulder blades together.

◢ Hold for a second before lowering.

AQUAMAN

◢ Lie on your front with your arms stretched out in front of you.

◢ Raise your left arm and right leg, keeping them both straight.

◢ Hold for a second and then lower them, while at the same time raising your right arm and left leg.

◢ Alternate sides in a swimming motion.

GYM BALL BACK EXTENSION

◢ Lie on a gym ball so it is beneath your abdomen.

◢ Keep your feet apart for balance and don't let them raise off the floor.

◢ Touch your fingers to your temples and curl your body around the ball.

◢ Lift your shoulders until your body forms a straight line – don't over-extend your spine.

INCLINE BENCH DUMB-BELL REVERSE FLYE

◢ Set the bench to between 30˚ and 45˚.

◢ Lie face-down and hold dumb-bells with your palms facing each other.

◢ Keeping a slight bend in your elbows, raise your arms in an arc to the sides.

◢ At the top of the move, squeeze your shoulder blades together and then lower slowly.

GYM BALL SUPINE REACH

◢ Lie on a gym ball so your head and shoulders are supported.

◢ Hold your body horizontal and place your feet apart on the floor so that your knees form a 90˚ angle.

◢ Point one arm to the ceiling while pressing your other upper arm into the ball.

◢ Push down on your bent arm and reach up to the ceiling with your straight arm, using your back and core muscles to get the maximum movement upwards.

FORM GUIDES

PULL-UP

The ultimate bodyweight exercise, the pull-up targets your back, lats and biceps, and is a true test of strength.

◢ Overhand grip.

◢ Grip the bar just wider than shoulder-width.

◢ Hang at full arm's length to start, and lower all the way down with each rep.

◢ Draw your shoulder blades down and together before you pull up.

◢ Hold your core muscles tight throughout the exercise.

◢ Cross your feet or hold your legs together.

◢ Pull up until your chin is level with the bar.

◢ Squeeze your shoulder blades at the top of the move.

◢ Don't raise your legs or swing your body to gain momentum as you lift.

◢ Lower as slowly as you can manage.

ALSO TRY

CHIN-UP

An underhand grip places more emphasis on your biceps

FORM GUIDES

SHOULDER PRESS

Also called the military press, this is the standard exercise for building bigger shoulders.

Head up, looking forward.

Hold the bar on your upper chest.

Press the bar directly overhead.

Stand up straight with your core braced.

Grip the bar just outside your shoulders with straight wrists.

Elbows out to your sides.

Feet apart for stability.

Keep your torso still – don't push your hips forward to get momentum.

12 MINUTE WORKOUT

ONE-LEG CURL TO PRESS

◢ Stand on one leg with your body upright.

◢ Curl the dumb-bells up to your chest, keeping your elbows close to your sides.

◢ Press the weights overhead, turning your wrists as you go.

◢ Reverse the move to the start.

ALTERNATING SHOULDER PRESS

◢ Hold dumb-bells at shoulder-height with your elbows out to the sides, palms facing forward.

◢ Press one of the weights directly overhead.

◢ As you lower it, press the other one up.

◢ Alternate sides with each rep.

PUSH PRESS

◢ Follow a similar form to the shoulder press.

◢ Before you lift, unlock your knees and drop into a shallow squat.

◢ As you push up with your legs, press the bar directly overhead – the added momentum will allow you to press heavier weights.

FORM GUIDES

INTERNAL ROTATION

◢ Stand side-on to a stretch band that has been attached to a solid object at waist-height.

◢ Grip the handle so your arm forms a 90° angle with your forearm pointing horizontally out to the side.

◢ Rotate your arm inwards, keeping your upper arm vertical.

EXTERNAL ROTATION

◢ Stand side-on to a stretch band that has been attached to a solid object at waist-height.

◢ Grip the handle with the arm furthest from the band, keeping your upper arm vertical and lower arm horizontal across your body.

◢ Rotate your arm outwards from your body with your elbow tucked at your side.

LATERAL RAISE

◢ Stand up straight, holding dumb-bells in front of you with your palms facing each other.

◢ Keeping a slight bend in your elbows, raise your arms in an arc out to the sides until they reach shoulder level.

◢ Pause for a second at the highest point and then lower the weights as slowly as you can.

DUMB-BELL HIGH PULL

◢ Hold dumb-bells in front of your thighs with your palms facing back.

◢ Unlock your knees and bend forward at the hips, keeping your back straight.

◢ Pull the dumb-bells up in front of you in a dynamic movement, leading with your elbows.

◢ Rise up onto your toes to get more momentum into the move.

◢ Squeeze your traps at the top of the move and then return to the start in a controlled manner.

BARBELL SHRUG

◢ Hold a heavy barbell in front of your thighs with an overhand grip.

◢ Keep your body upright and your core muscles braced.

◢ Without moving any other part of your body, lift your shoulders up towards your ears.

◢ Squeeze your traps at the top of the move and then return to the start in a controlled manner.

FORM GUIDES

PRESS-UP

A classic bodyweight move, the press-up tests your chest, triceps, shoulders and core.

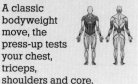

▲ Brace your core muscles and hold your body in a straight line from head to heels – don't let your hips sag.

▲ Feet close together to make your core work harder at stabilising your body.

▲ Hands just wider than shoulder-width apart.

▲ Hands beneath shoulders.

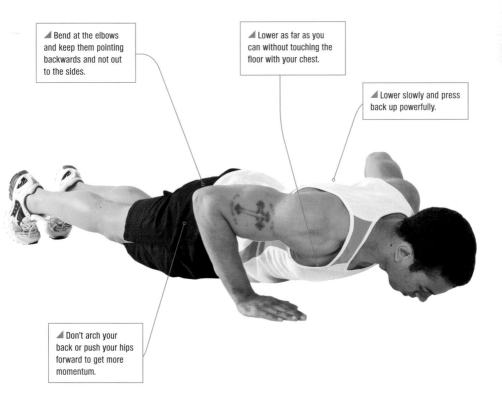

◢ Bend at the elbows and keep them pointing backwards and not out to the sides.

◢ Lower as far as you can without touching the floor with your chest.

◢ Lower slowly and press back up powerfully.

◢ Don't arch your back or push your hips forward to get more momentum.

FORM GUIDES

DUMB-BELL PRESS-UP

◢ Get into a press-up position (see form on previous page) holding dumb-bells with straight wrists.

◢ The extra height allows you to go deeper on the lowering portion of the exercise for more effective results.

MEDICINE BALL PRESS-UP

◢ Get into a press-up position (see form on previous page), but with both hands on a medicine ball and your feet apart for stability.

◢ Lower your chest to the ball, keeping your elbows close to your body.

MEDICINE BALL PASSING PRESS-UP

◢ Start in a press up position with one hand on a medicine ball.

◢ Keep your body in a straight line.

◢ You may need to take a wide stance to help maintain balance.

◢ Lower your body as far as you can and, as you rise up, roll the ball towards the other hand.

◢ Place your other hand on the ball and perform another press up before rolling it back again.

◢ Swap sides with each press up.

T PRESS-UP

◢ Get into a press up position but with a wider stance for balance.

◢ As you push up, lift one hand off the floor and rotate your torso until you can point towards the ceiling.

◢ Alternate sides with each rep.

PLYO OFFSET PRESS-UP

◢ Start in a press-up position, but with one hand further forward than your shoulders and one further back.

◢ Lower your chest towards the floor, then push up with enough force to lift your hands off the floor.

◢ In mid-air swap the position of your hands and go straight into the next press up as you land.

◢ Keep moving your hands backwards and forwards with each rep.

GYM BALL PRESS-UP

◢ Get into a press-up position, but with your feet resting on a gym ball.

◢ Keeping a straight back, lower your nose towards the floor and then push up while trying to minimise the wobble of the gym ball.

BENCH PRESS

The bench press is the king of upper-body moves, working your chest, shoulders and triceps together.

◢ Grip the bar just wider than shoulder-width apart.

◢ Keep your core muscles engaged throughout.

◢ Hold the bar directly above your chest.

◢ Feet flat on the floor for stability.

◢ Head and shoulders supported by the bench.

◢ Maintain the natural arch in your back.

◢ Lower the bar slowly to just above your chest, then press back up again powerfully.

◢ Don't lift your hips off the bench as you press the bar back up.

◢ Elbows to the sides.

GYM BALL ALTERNATING CHEST PRESS

◢ Lie on a gym ball with your head and shoulders supported, and your body in a straight line with knees bent at 90˚.

◢ Hold dumb-bells at chest-height with your elbows out to the sides.

◢ As you press one weight straight up, lower the other one, alternating with each rep.

DUMB-BELL INCLINE BENCH PRESS

◢ Set a bench at around 45˚ and sit with your back and head supported.

◢ Hold dumb-bells at chest-height with your palms facing forward and elbows out to the sides.

◢ Press the weights vertically upwards and then lower slowly to the start.

DUMB-BELL BENCH FLYE

◢ Lie on a flat bench with your head supported and feet flat on the floor.

◢ Hold dumb-bells above your chest with palms facing each other.

◢ Keeping a slight bend in your elbows, lower the weights slowly to the side in an arc, before squeezing your chest muscles and returning to the start.

FORM GUIDES

SHADOW BOXING

◢ This exercise emulates boxing moves to give you a cardio workout.

◢ Get into a boxing stance with feet apart and fists by your chin.

◢ Throw jabs, crosses, hooks and uppercuts with both hands – the aim is to keep moving and stay balanced on your feet.

JABS

◼ Hold dumb-bells at shoulder-height with palms facing in.

◼ Throw a punch out quickly with one hand, turning the palm to face down.

◼ Swap sides with each rep and twist your torso into each jab to get more power behind it.

UPPERCUTS

◢ Stand up straight holding dumb-bells at waist-height.

◢ Twist your torso to one side, rising up on your back foot, and perform an uppercut movement with the dumb-bell.

◢ Alternate sides with each rep, aiming to make each uppercut fast, powerful and controlled.

12 MINUTE WORKOUT

JUMPING JACKS

◢ Stand with your arms by your sides.

◢ Jump, moving your feet apart and raising your arms over your head at the same time.

◢ Jump back to the start and repeat, making your movements fast and controlled.

SQUAT THRUSTS

◢ Start in a press-up position with your body straight and your hands beneath your shoulders.

◢ Jump your feet forward, so your knees come up to your chest, and then jump your feet back to the start.

◢ Repeat quickly and under control.

HILL CLIMBERS

◢ From a press-up position, bring one knee in close to your chest.

◢ Jump that leg back while bringing the other one forward – a bit like running on the spot.

◢ Repeat quickly and under control.

FORM GUIDES

RUSSIAN TWIST

This move builds a strong core and improves sporting performance.

◢ Hold the weight straight out in front of you at chest-height.

◢ Keep your back upright and your core muscles braced.

◢ Feet just wider than shoulder-width apart.

MEDICINE BALL RUSSIAN TWIST

12
MINUTE
WORKOUT

Rotate your torso to one side keeping your back upright.

Alternate sides with fast, powerful, controlled movements.

Use your core muscles to accelerate and decelerate the weight as you rotate.

Rise up onto your back foot as you turn.

FORM GUIDES

BARBELL ROTATION

◢ Follow same the form as the Russian Twist on the previous page.

◢ Hold a barbell across the back of your shoulders – not your neck.

◢ Stand upright and use your core muscles to control the rotation of the bar.

LOWER-BODY ROTATION

◢ Lie on your back with your arms out to the sides for support.

◢ Hold your thighs vertical with your knees bent at 90˚.

◢ Rotate your lower body to one side until your knees almost touch the floor, and then return to the start and repeat on the other side.

◢ Keep your shoulders on the floor at all times.

ALSO TRY

STRAIGHT LEG LOWER-BODY ROTATION

GYM BALL RUSSIAN TWIST

◢ Lie on a gym ball with your head and shoulders supported, your feet on the floor and body held in a straight line.

◢ Hold a dumb-bell above your chest, keeping your arms straight.

◢ Rotate your torso to one side, allowing the ball to roll under you.

◢ Use your core muscles to control the rate of rotation.

DUMB-BELL SEATED RUSSIAN TWIST

◢ Sit on the floor and hold your torso at around 45° to the floor, keeping a straight back.

◢ Keep your legs slightly bent and out in front of you for balance.

◢ Hold a dumb-bell in front of your chest and rotate your torso from side to side while maintaining the angle of your back.

ALSO TRY

MEDICINE BALL SEATED RUSSIAN TWIST

FORM GUIDES

WOODCHOP

This move works multiple muscle groups through several different planes to provide real-world strength.

◢ Keep your back straight and core muscles braced throughout.

◢ Keep your arms straight as you pull them up and across your body.

◢ Stand side-on to a stretch band attached to a solid object at floor level.

◢ Turn your body towards the band.

◢ Maintain a strong core and rotate around the vertical axis.

◢ Bend your knees and swivel on your toes towards the band.

◢ Keep tension on the band at all times.

◢ Stand up and twist on your feet so that you rise up on your back toes.

12 MINUTE WORKOUT

JUDO THROW

◢ Stand side-on to a stretch band attached at shoulder-height.

◢ Start with tension on the band and twist away from it, bringing the handle over your shoulder.

◢ With the handle held at your chest, crunch forward using your abs to pull the band further down.

DUMB-BELL SIDE LUNGE WOODCHOP

◢ Stand up straight with feet together and a dumb-bell held over one shoulder.

◢ Take a step to the side with both feet pointing forward and bring the dumb-bell down and across your body in a chopping motion.

◢ Keep your back straight and core tight as you rotate your torso.

MEDICINE BALL LUNGE CHOP

◢ Stand up straight with a medicine ball held over one shoulder.

◢ Take a big step forward into a lunge, leading with the leg on the opposite side to the ball.

◢ At the same time, bring the ball down and across your body in a chopping motion.

◢ Keep your body upright throughout.

WEIGHTED
CRUNCH

The crunch is the standard move for training your abs. Adding weight allows you to work to a specific rep range.

◢ Hold a weight plate or dumb-bell against your chest.

◢ Knees bent and feet flat on the floor.

◢ Hold your head off the floor at the start.

◢ Use a mat to protect your lower back.

◢ Lift your shoulders off the floor and curl your chest towards your knees.

◢ Head in line with your torso.

◢ Squeeze your abdominal muscles and aim to hold the top position for a second before lowering slowly.

◢ Keep your lower back in contact with the mat.

FORM GUIDES

PUNCH UP CRUNCH

▲ Lie on the mat with knees bent and feet flat on the floor.

▲ Hold dumb-bells at chest-level.

▲ Crunch up and punch out with one of the weights up and across your body.

▲ Alternate sides with each rep.

CRUNCH THROW

▲ Hold a medicine ball to your chest.

▲ Sit up powerfully, raising your shoulders and lower back off the mat.

▲ As you come up, throw the ball away from you to a partner or against a wall.

▲ Catch the rebound and lower back to the start.

HANGING KNEE RAISE

▲ Hang from a pull-up bar with legs bent and feet crossed or together.

▲ Draw your knees up to your chest, using your abs to gain as much height as you can.

▲ Hold the top position for a second before lowering slowly.

▲ Don't swing to gain momentum.

BICYCLES

◢ Lie on the mat and touch your fingers to your temples.

◢ Hold your feet off the floor.

◢ Bring one knee back towards your chest and, at the same time, lift the opposite shoulder off the floor and twist your torso to bring your elbow to touch your knee.

◢ Twist back and forth, pumping your legs and touching your elbows to your knees.

◢ Use your abs to control the motion.

GYM BALL TWISTING CRUNCH

◢ Lie back on a gym ball with it beneath your lower back.

◢ Keep your feet on the floor.

◢ Touch your fingers to your temples and lean right back on the ball to get the full range of motion.

◢ Lift your shoulders up and crunch your chest towards your knees, twisting your torso to one side.

◢ Return slowly to the start and then repeat on the other side.

FORM GUIDES

PLANK

For building core stability and protecting your spine, the simple plank is a must-do exercise.

◢ Keep your body in a straight line from head to heels – don't let your hips sag.

◢ The wider apart your feet are, the more stable you become. Keep your feet close together to make your core work harder.

◢ Your elbows should be directly beneath your shoulders.

12 MINUTE WORKOUT

◢ Lock your shoulders into position so they are aligned and not hunched.

◢ Keep your head in line with your spine – don't over-extend your neck.

◢ Hold the position for as long as you can, and stop when you can no longer maintain good form.

FORM GUIDES

GYM BALL PLANK

◢ Rest your forearms on a gym ball, keeping your elbows beneath your shoulders.

◢ Hold your body in a straight line.

◢ Keep your feet apart for stability.

◢ Aim to hold the position for as long as possible while minimising the wobble of the gym ball.

GLUTE BRIDGE

◢ Lie on your back with knees bent and feet flat on the floor.

◢ Hold your arms by your sides for support.

◢ Raise your hips until your body forms a straight line from knees to shoulders.

◢ Hold for two to three seconds before lowering slowly.

ALSO TRY

GLUTE BRIDGE WITH LEG RAISE

As you raise your hips, extend one leg in line with your body.

SIDE BRIDGE

◢ Lie on your side with your elbow beneath your shoulder.

◢ Raise your hips until your body forms a straight line from head to heels.

◢ Hold the position for two to three seconds before lowering slowly.

PRONE STRETCH BAND PULLS

◢ Attach a stretch band to a solid object at floor level.

◢ Get in to a press-up position facing the band, but far enough from it that there is tension on the band when you hold the handle.

◢ Use your core muscles to maintain the press-up position while you draw the band back in a series of different motions.

◢ Pull the handle into your abdomen, then draw it out to the side with a straight arm, then pull it beneath you or overhead. You can mix up movements as you see fit.

SIDE PLANK WITH LATERAL RAISE

◢ Get into a side plank position with your elbow beneath your shoulder and body in a straight line.

◢ Hold a dumb-bell in your upper arm and raise and lower it slowly in front of your body without compromising your plank position.

TURKISH GET-UP

◢ Lie on the floor with your left knee bent and left arm pointing straight up.

◢ The aim of the exercise is to get from lying to standing while pointing upwards constantly.

◢ Start by rising onto your elbow.

◢ Lift your hips and push up onto one hand so that your body forms a straight line from head to toe.

◢ Bring your unsupported leg beneath you and place your toes on the floor behind you.

◢ Push up into a lunge position, still pointing upwards.

◢ Now stand up and bring your feet together before reversing the movement back to the beginning.

◢ Keep your core braced throughout, and make all your movements slow and deliberate.

PRESS-UP TO BURPEE TO CLEAN TO PRESS

◢ Holding dumb-bells, perform a press-up before jumping your feet forward beneath your chest.

◢ Rock back onto your heels and hold the weights at shin-height with a straight back and tight core.

◢ Pull the weights up in front of you and when they reach chest-height, drop into a squat and flip the weights over to catch them on your palms.

◢ Press the dumb-bells overhead.

◢ Reverse the move to the start.

MEDICINE BALL PRESS-UP TO BURPEE TO OVERHEAD SQUAT

◢ With your hands on a medicine ball, perform a press-up and then jump your feet forward beneath your chest.

◢ Grab the ball and stand up, lifting the ball above your head.

◢ Keep your back straight and core braced as you lift the ball.

◢ With the ball over your head, lower into a squat, keeping your torso upright and your knees in line with your feet.

◢ Reverse the move back to the start.

FORM GUIDES

CALF RAISES

◢ Stand on the edge of a box or step and use a wall for balance.

◢ Hold a dumb-bell in your other hand.

◢ Lower your heel as far as you can.

◢ Push up onto your toes and hold the position for a second before lowering slowly.

INCH WORM

◢ Start in a press-up position with your body straight and hands beneath your shoulders.

◢ Walk your feet forwards, taking small steps until your body forms an inverted 'V' shape.

◢ Now walk your hands forward until you return to the press up position.

◢ Repeat the movement pattern so that you move forwards slowly across the room.

◢ Keep your back flat and core braced throughout.

BARBELL BICEPS CURL

◢ Stand up straight with your shoulders back and core braced.

◢ Hold a barbell either side of your thighs in an underhand grip.

◢ Curl the bar up chest-height, keeping your elbows tucked close to your sides.

◢ Squeeze your biceps at the top and lower the bar slowly to the start.

◢ Don't lift your elbows or rock your body to gain extra momentum.

INCLINE BENCH DUMB-BELL BICEPS CURLS

◢ Set the bench at 45° and sit with your head supported and feet on the floor.

◢ Hold two dumb-bells with palms facing forward and your arms hanging straight down.

◢ Curl the weights up as far as you can without lifting your elbows.

DUMB-BELL LYING TRICEPS PRESS

◢ Lie on a flat bench and hold a dumb-bell in both hands over your head with your arms tilted back slightly.

◢ Keeping your upper arms in the same place, bend your elbows to lower the weight and then press back to the start by squeezing your triceps.

FORM GUIDES

GYM BALL LEG CURL

◢ Lie with your head and shoulders on the floor and heels on a gym ball.

◢ Hold your body in a straight line and keep your arms by your sides for stability.

ALSO TRY

GYM BALL HIP RAISE TO LEG CURL

Start with your back on the floor and raise your hips to begin the move.

◢ Draw the ball in towards your backside and raise your hips.

◢ Move the ball back and forth, using your hamstrings and core muscles to control the ball's movement.

GYM BALL JACKKNIFE

◢ Get into a press-up position with your hands beneath your shoulders and feet on a gym ball.

◢ Hold your body in a straight line.

ALSO TRY

GYM BALL TWISTING JACKKNIFE

Push your knees out to the sides as you draw the ball in.

◢ Pull your knees into your chest, rolling your feet over the ball as you move.

◢ Use your abs and hips to control the ball's motion.

MEDICINE BALL THROW DOWNS

◢ Take a wide stance and hold a medicine ball in front of you.

◢ Lift the ball over your head to your full extension and then throw it down in front of you as hard as you can.

◢ Make your movements fast and dynamic.

◢ Catch the ball on the bounce and repeat – note that some balls can bounce very high so it might be best to try this one outside.

MEDICINE BALL SLEDGEHAMMER

◢ Take a wide stance and hold a medicine ball between your legs.

◢ Keep your back straight and core braced.

◢ Bend at the knees and push your backside out.

◢ Stand up powerfully, pushing your hips forward, and lift the ball over your head in a swinging motion.

◢ Use your abs to decelerate the ball at the top of the move, and then bring it back down powerfully to the start.

Exercises by body part

BICEPS

Barbell biceps curl	125
Chin-up	94
Incline bench dumb-bell biceps curls	125
Lunge to curl	80
One-leg curl to press	97
Prone stretch band pulls	121
Pull-up	94
Squat to biceps curl	77
Squat to curl to press	77

TRICEPS

Bench press	104
Dumb-bell incline bench press	105
Dumb-bell lying triceps press	125
Dumb-bell press-up	102
Gym ball alternating chest press	105
Gym ball press-up	103
Medicine ball passing press-up	102
Medicine ball press-up	102
Medicine ball press-up to burpee to overhead squat	123
Plyo offset press-up	103
Press-up	100
Press-up to burpee to clean to press	123
Romanian deadlift to bent over row	88
T press-up	103

SHOULDERS

Alternating shoulder press	97
Crunch throw	116
External rotation	98
Hill climbers	107
Inch worm	124
Internal rotation	98
Jabs	106
Lateral raise	98
Medicine ball lunge chop	113
Medicine ball press-up to burpee to overhead squat	123
Medicine ball sledgehammer	127
Medicine ball throw downs	127

One-leg curl to press	97
Press-up to burpee to clean to press	123
Punch up crunch	116
Push press	97
Shoulder press	96
Side lunge woodchop	113
Side plank with lateral raise	121
Squat thrusts	107
Squat to curl to press	77
Squat to press	77
Squat to rotating shoulder press	77
Turkish get-up	122
Uppercuts	106
Woodchop	112

CHEST

Bench press	104
Crunch throw	116
Dumb-bell bench flye	105
Dumb-bell incline bench press	105
Dumb-bell press-up	102
Gym ball alternating chest press	105
Gym ball press-up	103
Jabs	106
Medicine ball passing press-up	102
Medicine ball press-up	102
Medicine ball press-up to burpee to overhead squat	123
Plyo offset press-up	103
Press-up	100
Press-up to burpee to clean to press	123

Punch up crunch	116
Shadow boxing	106
Split squat to one-arm press	85
T press-up	103
Uppercuts	106

BACK

Aquaman	92
Barbell shrug	99
Bent over row	90
Chin-up	95
Dorsal raise with shoulder rotation	92
Dumb-bell high pull	99
Dumb-bell incline bench row	91
Dumb-bell split deadlift to rear flye	88
Gym ball back extension	92
Gym ball prone alternating row	91
Gym ball supine reach	93
Incline bench dumb-bell reverse flye	93
Medicine ball sledgehammer	127
Press-up to burpee to clean to press	123
Prone stretch band pulls	121
Pull-up	94
Single-leg deadlift to row	89

Split Romanian deadlift to rear flye	88
Split squat to one-arm row	85
Squat to high pull	76
Renegade row	91
Romanian deadlift to bent over row	88
Turkish get-up	122

12 MINUTE WORKOUT